Photographic Memories

Francis Frith's
BRIDPORT

Rodney Legg

First published in the United Kingdom in 2001 by
The Francis Frith Collection

Paperback Edition 2001
ISBN 1-85937-327-5

British Library Cataloguing in Publication Data

Francis Frith's Bridport
Rodney Legg

The Francis Frith Collection
Frith's Barn, Teffont,
Salisbury, Wiltshire SP3 5QP
Tel: +44 (0) 1722 716 376
Email: info@francisfrith.co.uk
www.francisfrith.com

Printed and bound in Great Britain

Front Cover: Bridport, West Street 1913 65644

Contents

Francis Frith: *Victorian Pioneer*

FRANCIS FRITH, Victorian founder of the world-famous photographic archive, was a complex and multi-talented man. A devout Quaker and a highly successful Victorian businessman, he was both philosophic by nature and pioneering in outlook.

By 1855 Francis Frith had already established a wholesale grocery business in Liverpool, and sold it for the astonishing sum of £200,000, which is the equivalent today of over £15,000,000. Now a multi-millionaire, he was able to indulge his passion for travel. As a child he had pored over travel books written by early explorers, and his fancy and imagination had been stirred by family holidays to the sublime mountain regions of Wales and Scotland. 'What a land of spirit-stirring and enriching scenes and places!' he had written. He was to return to these scenes of grandeur in later years to 'recapture the thousands of vivid and tender memories', but with a different purpose. Now in his thirties, and captivated by the new science of photography, Frith set out on a series of pioneering journeys to the Nile regions that occupied him from 1856 until 1860.

Intrigue and Adventure

He took with him on his travels a specially-designed wicker carriage that acted as both dark-room and sleeping chamber. These far-flung journeys were packed with intrigue and adventure. In his life story, written when he was sixty-three, Frith tells of being held captive by bandits, and of fighting 'an awful midnight battle to the very point of surrender with a deadly pack of hungry, wild dogs'. Sporting flowing Arab costume, Frith arrived at Akaba by camel seventy years before Lawrence, where he encountered 'desert princes and rival sheikhs, blazing with jewel-hilted swords'.

During these extraordinary adventures he was assiduously exploring the desert regions bordering the Nile and patiently recording the antiquities and peoples with his camera. He was the first photographer to venture beyond the sixth cataract. Africa was still the mysterious 'Dark Continent', and Stanley and Livingstone's historic meeting was a decade into the future. The conditions for picture taking confound belief. He laboured for hours in his wicker dark-room in the sweltering heat of the desert, while the volatile chemicals fizzed dangerously in their trays. Often he was forced to work in remote tombs and caves where conditions were cooler. Back in London he exhibited his photographs and was 'rapturously cheered' by members of the Royal Society. His reputation as a photographer was made overnight. An eminent modern historian has likened his impact on the population of the time to that on our own generation of the first photographs taken on the surface of the moon.

Venture of a Life-Time

Characteristically, Frith quickly spotted the opportunity to create a new business as a specialist publisher of photographs. He lived in an era of immense and sometimes violent change. For the poor in the early part of Victoria's reign work was a drudge and the hours long, and people had precious little free time to enjoy themselves. Most had no transport other than a cart or gig at their disposal, and had not travelled far beyond the boundaries of their own town or village. However, by the 1870s, the railways had threaded their way across the country, and Bank Holidays and half-day Saturdays had been made obligatory by Act of Parliament. All of a sudden the ordinary working man and his family were able to enjoy days out and see a little more of the world.

With characteristic business acumen, Francis Frith foresaw that these new tourists would enjoy having souvenirs to commemorate their days out. In 1860 he married Mary Ann Rosling and set out with the intention of photographing every city, town and village in Britain. For the next thirty years he travelled the country by train and by pony and trap, producing fine photographs of seaside resorts and beauty spots that were keenly bought by millions of Victorians. These prints were painstakingly pasted into family albums and pored over during the dark nights of winter, rekindling precious memories of summer excursions.

The Rise of Frith & Co

Frith's studio was soon supplying retail shops all over the country. To meet the demand he gathered about him a small team of photographers, and published the work of independent artist-photographers of the calibre of Roger Fenton and Francis Bedford. In order to gain some understanding of the scale of Frith's business one only has to look at the catalogue issued by Frith & Co in 1886: it runs to some 670 pages, listing not only many thousands of views of the British Isles but also many photographs of most European countries, and China, Japan, the USA and Canada – note the sample page shown above from the hand-written *Frith & Co* ledgers detailing pictures taken. By 1890 Frith had created the greatest specialist photographic publishing company in the

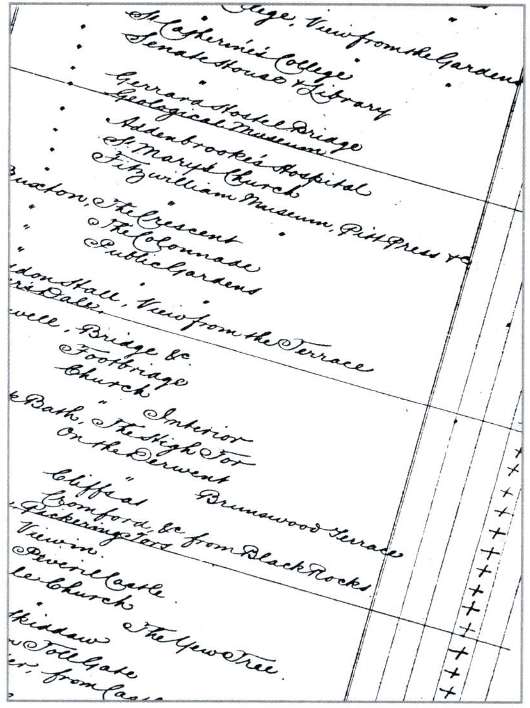

world, with over 2,000 outlets – more than the combined number that Boots and WH Smith have today! The picture on the right shows the *Frith & Co* display board at Ingleton in the Yorkshire Dales. Beautifully constructed with mahogany frame and gilt inserts, it could display up to a dozen local scenes.

Postcard Bonanza

The ever-popular holiday postcard we know today took many years to develop. In 1870 the Post Office issued the first plain cards, with a pre-printed stamp on one face. In 1894 they allowed other publishers' cards to be sent through the mail with an attached adhesive halfpenny stamp. Demand grew rapidly, and in 1895 a new size of postcard was permitted called the court card, but there was little room for illustration. In 1899, a year after

Frith's death, a new card measuring 5.5 x 3.5 inches became the standard format, but it was not until 1902 that the divided back came into being, with address and message on one face and a full-size illustration on the other. *Frith & Co* were in the vanguard of postcard development, and Frith's sons Eustace and Cyril continued their father's monumental task, expanding the number of views offered to the public and recording more and more places in Britain, as the coasts and countryside were opened up to mass travel.

Francis Frith died in 1898 at his villa in Cannes, his great project still growing. The archive he created continued in business for another seventy years. By 1970 it contained over a third of a million pictures of 7,000 cities, towns and villages. The massive photographic record Frith has left to us stands as a living monument to a special and very remarkable man.

Frith's Archive: *A Unique Legacy*

FRANCIS FRITH'S legacy to us today is of immense significance and value, for the magnificent archive of evocative photographs he created provides a unique record of change in 7,000 cities, towns and villages throughout Britain over a century and more. Frith and his fellow studio photographers revisited locations many times down the years to update their views, compiling for us an enthralling and colourful pageant of British life and character.

We tend to think of Frith's sepia views of Britain as nostalgic, for most of us use them to conjure up memories of places in our own lives with which we have family associations. It often makes us forget that to Francis Frith they were records of daily life as it was actually being lived in the cities, towns and villages of his day. The Victorian age was one of great and often bewildering change for ordinary people, and though the pictures evoke an impression of slower times, life was as busy and hectic as it is today.

We are fortunate that Frith was a photographer of the people, dedicated to recording the minutiae of everyday life. For it is this sheer wealth of visual data, the painstaking chronicle of changes in dress, transport, street layouts, buildings, housing, engineering and landscape that captivates us so much today. His remarkable images offer us a powerful link with the past and with the lives of our ancestors.

Today's Technology

Computers have now made it possible for Frith's many thousands of images to be accessed almost instantly. In the Frith archive today, each photograph is carefully 'digitised' then stored on a CD Rom. Frith archivists can locate a single photograph amongst thousands within seconds. Views can be catalogued and sorted under a variety of categories of place and content to the immediate benefit of researchers.

Inexpensive reference prints can be created for them at the touch of a mouse button, and a wide range of books and other printed materials assembled and published for a wider, more general readership - in the next twelve months over a hundred Frith local history titles will be published! The day-to-day workings of the archive are very different from how they were in Francis Frith's time: imagine the herculean task of sorting through eleven tons of glass negatives as Frith had to do to locate a particular sequence of pictures! Yet the

See Frith at www.francisfrith.co.uk

archive still prides itself on maintaining the same high standards of excellence laid down by Francis Frith, including the painstaking cataloguing and indexing of every view.

It is curious to reflect on how the internet now allows researchers in America and elsewhere greater instant access to the archive than Frith himself ever enjoyed. Many thousands of individual views can be called up on screen within seconds on one of the Frith internet sites, enabling people living continents away to revisit the streets of their ancestral home town, or view places in Britain where they have enjoyed holidays. Many overseas researchers welcome the chance to view special theme selections, such as transport, sports, costume and ancient monuments.

We are certain that Francis Frith would have heartily approved of these modern developments in imaging techniques, for he himself was always working at the very limits of Victorian photographic technology.

The Value of the Archive Today

Because of the benefits brought by the computer, Frith's images are increasingly studied by social historians, by researchers into genealogy and ancestory, by architects, town planners, and by teachers and schoolchildren involved in local history projects.

In addition, the archive offers every one of us an opportunity to examine the places where we and our families have lived and worked down the years. Highly successful in Frith's own era, the archive is now, a century and more on, entering a new phase of popularity.

The Past in Tune with the Future

Historians consider the Francis Frith Collection to be of prime national importance. It is the only archive of its kind remaining in private ownership and has been valued at a million pounds. However, this figure is now rapidly increasing as digital technology enables more and more people around the world to enjoy its benefits.

Francis Frith's archive is now housed in an historic timber barn in the beautiful village of Teffont in Wiltshire. Its founder would not recognize the archive office as it is today. In place of the many thousands of dusty boxes containing glass plate negatives and an all-pervading odour of photographic chemicals, there are now ranks of computer screens. He would be amazed to watch his images travelling round the world at unimaginable speeds through network and internet lines.

The archive's future is both bright and exciting. Francis Frith, with his unshakeable belief in making photographs available to the greatest number of people, would undoubtedly approve of what is being done today with his lifetime's work. His photographs, depicting our shared past, are now bringing pleasure and enlightenment to millions around the world a century and more after his death.

BRIDPORT - *An Introduction*

THE BRIDPORT OF the postcard photographer misses its main claim to fame. To be 'stabbed by a Bridport dagger' was to be hanged. There was particular local pleasure in 1778 when this became the fate of notorious highway robber Thomas Boulter who made his last call of "Stand and deliver" to the driver of the Salisbury coach on the Exeter road and was subsequently recognised and unmasked to the authorities by the landlord of the Castle Inn in Bridport.

A noose is hardly the image to send home from holiday, but neither is there anything here to remind us of industrial hemp, rope walks, sail-making and the 20th-century demand for military camouflage netting. Instead our photographers for the mass-market concentrate on street scenes from the town, on boats in the nearby harbour, and the rural idyll in the surrounding villages. There

we focus on four essentials that are as vital today as they were a century ago. In order to be a self-sufficient community a functioning village must have a parish church, public house, post office stores and a primary school. Not necessarily in that order perhaps, but the lesson of countryside change over the past few decades has been that from the moment one is lost, the others are also in peril. West Dorset would be hit as hard as anywhere in England by successive waves of redundant churches, delicensed inns, shut shops and closed schools.

Francis Frith's photographers had their commercial imperatives right when it came to the occasional detailed shop-front, as with the splendid shots of Wilfrid Frost's stationers in West Street, Bridport, and the Post Office in Main Street, Chideock. The photographer pictured the very places that would be selling Frith's postcards. Following up the scenes, by looking at the buildings and talking to residents, I discovered the amazing coincidence that the baby in the perambulator – pictured before the Great War – would, as Mrs Kathleen Symes, be the village postmistress for much of the remainder of the 20th century.

Electoral rolls and trade directories show that families such as Balson, Crabb, Gale, Gundry, Hine, Northover, Perrott, Pitfield, Rendell Samways and Legg, my own clan, also had their origins in the Bridport area. There is a hidden wealth of family history behind the photographs. The public houses proved as invaluable as the churches in providing identification clues and bringing continuity to span the decades.

Comparison between pictures shows that it was a time when inns were transforming themselves into hotels, though the locals were reluctant to add either to their names. There were dozens of places where you could enjoy a drink in Bridport and the surrounding countryside. Many public houses, clubs and their temperance alternatives were in business at the close of the Victorian age and through the Edwardian era.

There were also numerous beer retailers at the end of the Victorian age. Frederick Biles, Cornelius Dunn, John Kitcher, George Podger, William Scadding and Matthew Shearman were all in business in South Street, appropriately within yards of the brewery. Charles Albert Gale was in West Street. Levi Richard Gale was in West Bay Road. William John Gale and George Weeks were in Folly Mill Lane. Miss Rebecca Hart was in West Street. William Kingman serviced West Allington. Mrs Augusta Priest and Mrs Ann Warbin were in North Allington. John Samson had the net-workers in St Michael's Lane. Isaac Patten was in Barrack Street.

The other enduring theme is the landscape. Thankfully, primarily through the gifts of playwright R C Sherriff and public support of the Enterprise Neptune project in the 1960s, almost all the shoreline and much of the coastal hinterland between Eype and Charmouth came into National Trust ownership. This now extends for nine miles, incorporating all but the inhabited valleys westwards to Ware Cliffs, on Devonshire Head, beyond Lyme Regis. There is also a substantial Trust presence on the other side of West Bay, beyond West Dorset Golf Club, at Burton Cliff and Cogden Beach. Inland, the Trust protects a string of the key western heights including Hardown Hill, Lambert's Castle, Pilsdon Pen, Lewesdon Hill and Eggardon Hill. Closer to Bridport, the Woodland Trust owns the pine clump on Colmer's Hill, which forms a distinctive conical backdrop to many of our West Street views.

Identification has proved a pleasure and an endurance, depending upon the success rate, and Frith's filing has been awry on a few occasions. Residents galore have participated in the exercise and provided many of the anecdotes. Where nothing else has been found on the ground I have relied on their knowledge and wisdom for locational details.

Postcard views are quintessentially nostalgic. They are sent as a statement of affinity and approval. All the better if there are only anonymous distant figures, and minimal traffic, so we can pretend that we are not sharing the experience with the world and his wife. Where we can feel both relief and pride in reviewing a century's output is that so many of the settings remain largely unspoilt. Apocalyptic threats from caravan camps and intensive farming have almost failed to make a visual impact. Change elsewhere has been at the edges rather than the core. In the event of a revival of postcard-sending, these street scenes, the rugged coastline, and even inland landmarks can still be found in abundance to await the return of a Frith photographer. He may well stand at the very same spot as his predecessor.

Bridport Town

East Street 1897 40073
Here we are looking west along East Street, to the Town Hall and
Market Place. This was the retail hub of the town, with each blind
shadowing a shop window on the sunny northern side
of the exceptionally wide street. The gable-end signage is for
John J Shephard's Brush and Basket Manufactory and
William Shephard's Photographic Establishment. Opposite (far left)
the illuminated wines and spirits sign also offers Cyclists' Touring Club
Quarters. Further along are Louis Trevett's haircutting and shampooing
saloons. A ladder leans against the gutter beside Dick's Boots.

◀ **East Bridge 1897** 40080
East Bridge, at the eastern end of
East Street (left), was built by
J and T Gale in 1784 and has been
widened. This picture shows a mill
leat from the River Asker (right) and a
three storey building (left), the former
Marquis of Granby, which dates
from 1768. The 16th-century house
behind it is reputed to have been
the Hospital of St John the Baptist.
There is another 18th-century house
on the opposite side of the street,
built in 1769 as Rev James Rooker's
Academy (right). Looking westwards,
towards the King of Prussia, we can
see the cupola of the Town Hall in
the distance (centre).

East Street 1897 40074
This view shows the western end of East Street, with a closer look at the Town Hall clock-tower and cupola, and Colmer's Hill forming the conical eminence in the distance (centre). Shops on the south side include that of grocer and jam manufacturer William G Cornick. The Greyhound Hotel forms the penultimate frontage. Opposite the Old George Hotel is the premises of James Beach, pharmaceutical chemist and maker of the Poor Man's Friend ointment, with iron merchants and supplier of sewing machines H N Cox and Son next-door (fronted by lamp standards). Further along is the shopfront of ironmonger Gerard Alexander Samson.

East Street, Old Mill 1899 43865
Here we see East Mill and its mill pool, looking eastwards from the north bank of River Asker, towards houses beside East Road (centre). The Cottage, glimpsed behind the tree, stands beside Lower Walditch Road.

East Street 1902 48390
This view is of East Street, looking westwards to the Town Hall (left) with the prominent frontage of William Elmes, draper and outfitters, on the other side of the road (right). Beside it is the multi-panelled period frontage of grocer and Italian warehouseman John Alderton Collins. Trading directly opposite the Town Hall was ironmonger Charles Edward Bazley (centre).

East Street 1904
52756
This lively low-angle shot, virtually from ground level, looks north-eastwards along the Market Place and the northern side of East Street at its western end. Opposite, carrying the plate for South Street, is the Town Hall (right). Early Edwardian businesses extended from White's furnishing stores (far left) and the Markethouse Inn, followed by Charles Bazley's cycle shop and Hodder's Temperance Hotel. The awnings are over the furniture of William George Perrott and Sons. The historic decorative frontage of the former George Inn, which featured in the flight of King Charles II from the Battle of Worcester, carries the names of Beach the dispensing chemist, and predecessor Dr Roberts who produced patent medicines. Cox and Sons, ironmongers, are next.

East Bridge 1902 48393
Duplicating an earlier shot from 1897, this view is looking westwards up East Street from the River Asker and East Bridge. Virginia creeper has now spread to every inch of stonework on the 18th-century house (centre right). On the skyline, in the gap, are the three-storey lines of Grove House in Rax Lane (right). The public house sign (centre) is that of the King of Prussia.

East Street 1902 48391

Again we are looking west from the central part of East Street with the illuminated sign carrying the initials of the Cyclists' Touring Club (far left) having dropped its 'Wines and Spirits' in favour of 'Commercial Hotel'. On the street, a new generation had not yet been born in the Victorian shot, but otherwise not much has changed. Opposite are Guppy the grocers, the family business of William and Alfred Guppy (far right). Further along is another family concern, with brush and basket-maker John Shephard sharing a building with William and Annie Shephard, photographers.

East Street Station 1904
52757

This is East Bridge, at the eastern end of East Street (far right), looking eastwards from the north bank of the River Asker. The street becomes East Road and was gated with a level crossing (in front of the thatched cottage) for the West Bay extension of the Bridport Railway, in use from 1884 to 1962. Here the town had its own second halt, known as West Street Station, from the 1884 opening of the line until its closure in 1930. The trees (right) obscure stucco-fronted houses dating from about 1840.

East Mill 1904 52758

East Mill stood on the north side of East Road and was powered by the River Asker. This view, dating from 1904, looks eastwards from the north bank and duplicates picture 43865 on page 17.

▼ East Street 1912 65053

This picture was taken eastwards from the north side of East Street, from Mrs Alice E Gale's musical instrument emporium and fancy repository on the corner with Barrack Street (left). Not much else is visible in this otherwise largely shop-less scene before the Great War, when the eastern half of the main road – which would become the A35 with the creation of the strategic Folkestone to Honiton trunk road – was very much the town's secondary trading area.

▼ East Street 1927 79314

This looks westwards. Daimler taxis are parked outside the Bull Hotel (left) and the Town Hall clock is at noon (centre) which is borne out by shadows from the south and shop blinds shading the windows. Cars outnumber people in an otherwise quiet scene.

▲ East Street 1930 83340

This is another view westwards from opposite the Bull Hotel, with a sighting of Boy Scouts in hats (beside the lamp-post) and a pavement placard for Devonshire Cream Teas. On the other side (left of the cars) boot and shoe seller George Percival Read boasts 'Established 1844' and in the 1930s would be offering 'Moccasin', 'Norvic' and 'Mascot' brands. Johnson Bros, dyers, were next-door.

◄ **East Street 1937** 88010
The freedom of the road,
when roadside parking
was an inalienable right, can
be seen in a view westwards
to the Town Hall (centre)
from opposite the
Golden Rod Café (far left).
Prominent shop signs
include Frisby's shoe
stores (left of centre)
and photographer
Percy S Smith (right)
between a hairdressers
and P J King's Rax Dairy.
The front cars are a
Riley (left) and a Wolesley
(right).

DORSET DAILY ECHO
ADVERTISEMENTS RECEIVED
HINE & SON
FILMS
FILMS
SIGHT TESTED
JEWELLER J. TURNER
OPTICIAN
BOOKSELLERS | HINE & SON | STATIONERS
FRISBY'S BOOT STORES
FRISBY'S
GJ 6765

East Street 1930

83341

Detail abounds in this more intimate shot of the row of shops immediately east from the Town Hall and the Greyhound Hotel. All the windows are full of offerings from floor to ceiling. Secondary advertising is also prolific, with jeweller J Turner also being a 'Sight Tested' optician. Hine and Sons, booksellers and stationers, have canvas signs for 'Films' and earlier raised letters offering advertising services on behalf of the 'Dorset Daily Echo'. Frisby's is a boot store and Day and Son are general drapers. A Morris 18 (left) is parked behind an Austin 16 and PG 8782 (right) has 'GB' plates from a foreign tour.

East Street c1955 B207004
Deep shadows engulf the Greyhound Hotel (left), with the Town Hall behind, in this lunchtime view westwards to Colmer's Hill (centre). The board on the side of the Town Hall is for the Municipal Camping Ground. On the opposite side of East Street, beside the junction with Downes Street, a sign for the Soldiers Canteen and Recreation Room (right). The corner shop is that of Cox and Humphries, a hardware and sports store, with Boots the Chemist towards the Market Place.

East Street c1955 B207003
This photograph looks eastwards along East Street from the southern pavement, with the Midland Bank opposite (left). Next-door, the International Tea Company's Stores Limited has re-branded itself as the International Stores, and would remain a major grocery chain until the coming of purpose-built supermarkets. On the other side of the road, dispensing pharmacist N R Hilton is now trading as Hilton and Moss Chemists (right). The closest parked cars on each side are Humbers, with a Riley 9 further along the north side of the street (centre).

East Street c1965 B207047
A rare shot from a postcard cameraman in that it shows people, close-up and in motion, passing the photography sign for Leslie D Frisby (left). Next-door is the Packhorse Hotel. Beyond the Esso petrol logo of Stevenson's Garage are road signs, pointing into Barrack Street, for Beaminster and Crewkerne. Opposite, in a view eastwards towards Dorchester, is a bullish advertisement for W W Hoskins and Son, high class butchers: 'We buy and sell only the best'.

South Street 1897 40070
This is looking northwards up South Street, to Stag House at the top end of West Street and the Town Hall (centre). The town's main north-south thoroughfare was then largely residential with the only prominent shopfront being that of Turner's Corn and Seed Stores (left), advertising Lipton's Teas above the door. Street cleaners stand back from their wheelbarrows and a drayman delivers to the Ship Inn (right), with the Cross Keys and a striped barber's pole being glimpsed behind. John Hartgill, draper and outfitter, had his business in Stag House.

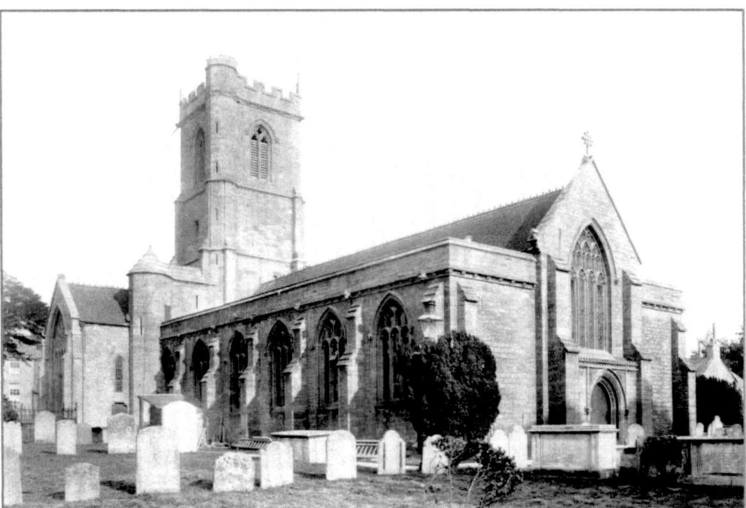

◀ **St Mary's Church 1897** 40077
This is St Mary's Parish church, seen from the north-west, showing the two bays of the nave and aisles extended in 1860 (right). The next four bays are from the previous extensions in the 15th century, when the central tower was also rebuilt, and the newel staircase added. It is set into the north-west wall of the surviving 13th-century transept of the original medieval design. The Victorian restoration began in 1859 and was carried out by ecclesiastical architect John Hicks of Dorchester, whose assistant draughtsman at this time was the young novelist Thomas Hardy.

◄ **South Street 1897** 40075
This looks Southwards along South Street to St Mary's parish church (centre). The east side begins with the projecting porch of the 16th-century building known as the Old Castle (far left), which is now Bridport Museum. Northover's Cheap Hardware Stores is the three-storey building. On the west side, between the figures and the church tower, is the establishment of draper and milliner Ernest Benjamin Hobbs. The office and works of Aldis Printers are to the right of those standing on the pavement.

▼ **Old Cottages 1897** 40095
Already falling into disrepair in Victorian times, thatched cottages on the east side of South Street, beside South Bridge, would soon succumb to the front-line of urbanisation. Here we are looking westwards, along the south bank of the River Asker, to the beginnings of the new suburb below Watton Cross.

◄ **St Mary's Parish Church 1902** 48395
This is St Mary's parish church in South Street, seen from the north-east. The projecting north transept (right) dates from the 13th century and is two centuries older than the tower. The remainder, with the nave flanked on either side by aisles, was rebuilt in 1860. It had only been intended to rebuild the outer walls but the project became much more ambitious. The rector in late Victorian and Edwardian times, from 1895, was Rev Henry Farrer.

St Mary's Rectory 1906 54541
The Rectory in South Street, on the south side of St Mary's parish church, was the home of the Rural Dean, Rev Henry Richard William Farrer, who was an honorary canon of Salisbury Cathedral. Here it is seen from the grounds, looking northwards, with the church tower beyond. Farrer's second son, Major Henry William Francis Blackburne Farrer of the Royal Field Artillery, would be killed at the age of 24 by a German shell in France, only days before the end of the Great War in 1918.

South Street 1912 65054
This photograph looks southwards along South Street from the Cross Keys (left) next to butcher Arthur Lewis and cycle agent Charles Frederick Fooks. The cart belonging to the former is moving off. Opposite were hatter and hosier Frederick W Dinham and grocer Samuel Douglas Whitemore. There is another cycle store along the street.

South Street 1927 79320
This scene was captured looking northwards to the Town Hall from
the pavement beside Bridport and District Co-Operative Society. The
bicycle (right) is outside Hallett and Son's cycle shop which advertises:
'Coventry Eagles Bicycles have just arrived. Yours today.
11 shillings.' Next-door is the Ship Inn with Bridport Electric Palace
being the adjacent cinema.

▼ **South Street c1955** B207016
Here we see the view southwards along South Street, from the taxi rank (left) to the tower of St Mary's parish church (right of centre). This was the B3157 to West Bay and Burton bradstock. The closest parked car is an Austin 12 (left).

▼ **South Street c1965** B207070
In contrast to the bustle of East Street, the southern length of South Street was very much a secondary shopping area. There are fewer people and fewer cars. Public transport has a presence, with a taxi rank (left) and the offices of Southern National Coaches (opposite). A Ford Zodiac is the closest parked car (left). Conspicuous businesses include A J Bedingfield, dispensing chemist (left), and the Wine Shop (right). The grocer on the other side of the road is Whitemore's Stores. The tower of St Mary's church is beyond the pedestrian crossing (centre).

▲ **West Street 1897** 40071
On the south side of this view is the London House store of house furnishers Walter Baker Northover and Son. Colmer's Hill is the distinctive distant hilltop (centre). On the north side of the street the confident commercial frontage is that of the Wilts and Dorset Bank, which was absorbed into Lloyds (right). Down the slope is the sign of the Royal Oak Hotel (above the hand-cart) and the shop window of butchers W and R Fletcher Limited (two ladies passing), with a painter on a ladder further down the hill.

◄ West Street 1902
48392

Here the photograph looks down West Street to Colmer's Hill (left), with the Lily Hotel projecting into the highway as it narrows to a normal width near the bottom of the hill. Rope-walks, weaving and trailing along the pavements, are said to be the reason why Bridport has such unusually wide streets. Opposite is the Royal Oak Hotel (centre), and the Wilts and Dorset Bank (far right) had yet to be absorbed into Lloyds.

West Street 1904 52755
Now we look westwards down the south side of West Street, from
Knight and Son, tailors (far left). The next building housed stationer
and printer W Frost who published the 'Bridport News'. Next is
the Sun Inn, followed by confectioner and milliner Miss Amanda
Spiller (with two separate shops), and Mrs Rosa Warren's china and
glass store. Best Outfitters are in the three-storey building, beyond
which the Lily Hotel projects towards the road, with Colmer's Hill
being the distinctive hilltop (centre).

West Street 1909 61645
This is the south side of West Street, from the north-east. W Frost, bookseller and publisher of the 'Bridport News',
was next-door to the Sun Hotel, where the landlord was William Kingman. The double shop-fronts of Miss Amanda
Spiller (confectioner through the left door, and milliner through the right) and Mrs Rosa Warren are followed by
outfitters Frederick W Best and Ernest R Best. In the distance, beyond the Lily Hotel, the White Lion Inn is the final
gable-end that can be seen.

W Frost Shop Front 1909 61645x
This is a detail of the frontage of 34 West Street, which was the 'Bridport News' office and West Dorset Printing
Works in 1909. Multi-talented W Frost advertised himself as stationer, printer, bookseller, bookbinder, newsagent,
and circulating library manager. He was also publisher and proprietor of the local newspaper, the full title of which
was the 'Bridport News & Dorset, Devon and Somerset Advertiser'. Wilfrid Frost lived at Glyn in Park Road.

West Street 1912 65051

Westwards up West Street to the Town Hall (left of centre), a Model-T Ford passes the shops of Best, Warren and Spiller (right). Their names are now familiar, as is that of William Kingman's Sun Hotel. The early car registration plate is FX115. 'FX' were Dorset's first letters, starting with FX 100, but 'BF' had been allocated to the county. The Lord Lieutenant protested to Whitehall: "If you pause for a moment to reflect what the military man in the street is going to think of my passing, then you will realise my hesitation at accepting the designation Bloody Fool One." So 'FX' was issued instead and 'BF' remained available for half a century, until Staffordshire accepted the letters without complaint. Barrack room swearing had obviously moved on by then.

West Street 1913 65644
This looks eastwards up West Street, with hand-carts and horse-carts, and plenty of activity in the Market Place, beside the Town Hall (right). Hurdles for animal pens are stacked behind the far trees. Market days were Wednesday and Saturday. Fairs, for cattle and cheese, took place on the first Wednesday in April and October.

West Street 1913 65643
This view depicts the bustle in West Street, with children and cycles, and a flock of sheep being driven uphill (left of centre). Market stalls for animals can be seen between the trees. In the centre is the Royal Oak Hotel and the Wilts and Dorset Bank. Next-door (right) Charles Edward Bazley offers Humber and Swift bicycles. His shop blind couples 'Cycle Depot' with 'Furniture, China and Glass'.

WILTS & DORSET BANK
BAZLEY
CYCLE DEPÔT
C. E. BAZLEY
FURNITURE CHINA GLASS
BAZLEY

THE GREYHOUND HOTEL
HOTEL
DANGEROUS
CORNER
ON LEFT
GREYHOUND HOTEL
OT-558
PR 2822

West Street 1930
83342
This is another closer view along West Street to the former Market Place, from the Greyhound hotel (left) which faces the wonderfully elaborate Georgian shop-front of Beach and Company. 'Late Dr Roberts' was the apothecary whose medicines were still being manufactured. Below the sign, a highlight of earlier history is recorded: "The Old George Inn. King Charles II came here September 23rd 1651." The Town Hall (top left) was designed by William Tyler in 1785. An Austin 7 Tourer (left) is parked in front of the Morris Commercial delivery van.

West Street 1927 79313
This is a view looking eastwards up West Street, along the south
side from the Sun Hotel (right) to the Town Hall cupola. Limes trees
(left) have been pruned into mop-head lollipops, confirming that this
is a winter photo, which also explains the heavy clothing. Cars are
becoming more common with a Standard 9 being the closest vehicle.

West Street 1937 88009

This shows pre-war motoring at its peak, moving both ways up and down West Street, which was the A35 main road. The shop beside TK 813 is W Frost (right), stationer, bookseller and printer, who still ran a circulating library. Further up the street (centre right) are signs for Roberts grocers and E Lewis, a glass and china dealer. A Morris 12 is parked beside the first lime tree (left) and a Riley 9 is parked beside the bus-stop (right of centre).

West Street c1955 B207018

A remarkably foreshortened shot, westwards down West Street, with the 1785-built arch (far left) being the north-west corner of the Town Hall. The road sign points down South Street which is almost invisible between the public building and the shops. Colmer's Hill (right of centre) forms the distant skyline. The Royal Oak is on the north side of the street (right). The busy mix of cyclists and cars is typical of a 1950s street scene. The closest cars are a Morris 10 (left) and a Standard 9 (right) with a Humber behind.

West Street c1965 B207077
This picture looks westwards down the north side of West Street, with its lollipop limes, from the Post Office to Victoria Grove (right of centre). A Jaguar XJ is emerging from this road into the main one as an Austin A40 Farina manoeuvres into a parking space on the other side (left). The projecting sign (right of centre) is for the Port Bredy Guest House. Opposite, under the Esso sign (left), Bridport Motor Company Ltd held dealerships for Morris, Daimler, Wolseley and Lanchester.

West Street c1965 B207078
The lower end of West Street, looking westwards, has all manner of public houses from the Sun Hotel (left) to the Lily Hotel. Between them are the showrooms of Bridport Motors. Opposite, the Port Bredy Guest House takes its name from that used for the town in the Wessex novels of Thomas Hardy. Victoria Grove branches off between the trees (right). Further down there is a Ford Corsair. Opposite a Ford Anglia is tightly parked (left) between a couple of Morris Minis.

West Allington
Allington 1897 40099

Bridport borough expanded north-westwards into Allington parish in 1835. Street names initially included 'Reform Place 1835' to commemorate electoral changes after the Boundary Commission had reported: "The chief trade arises from the manufacture of hemp and flax, and Allington appears to be the resort of the poorer class of the population engaged in these manufactures." By the time of Queen Victoria's diamond jubilee, when this picture was taken, fashionable Allington Park had been established cheek by jowl with artisan terraces. The boys are standing beside the junction of Park Road. The houses are Polly's and Clayhanger (left) and Stoke Lodge (centre) with the terraces being No 16 to No 6 (right).

From Allington Hill 1897 40068
The main street of Allington village (bottom left) leads into this panorama of Bridport
town, looking south-east from Allington Hill, with the outer parish's St Swithun's
Church being the prominent building (centre right). It was built in 1826, in a rare
Greek-revival style, with a circular bell tower above the pedimented Doric portico.
Beyond, stretching from right to left, is the line of West Street through to the
Town Hall and Market Place, with the chimneys of net-makers Joseph Gundry and
Company (centre left), Ewens and Turner in St Michael's Lane (centre), and the
Bridport Brewery (centre right). The distant tower (centre) is St Mary's parish church.
Beyond is North Hill, above Burton Bradstock, with the hills of Bothenhampton and
Hyde forming the eastern horizon (left).

St Swithun's Church 1897 40079
St Swithun's parish church at Allington, now in the north-west corner of the
extended Bridport borough, was consecrated in 1827 to replace the original
medieval church to the west of the Vicarage, in what is now Parsonage Road. The
new church was designed by Charles Wallis of Dorchester to a neo-Grecian design
with a Doric portico of Tuscan columns supporting the architrave, triglyphic frieze,
pediment and tympanum. The circular bell cupola has louvered openings on a
square base and is topped by an elliptical domed roof. Inside it is what was known
as a preaching church, with clergy and congregation sharing the same space,
rather than the former carrying out their rituals in a segregated chancel.

▼ **West Allington 1899** 43868

This view is looking westwards towards Symondsbury and Exeter along what was generally called the London Road, with a variety of hand-carts and a couple of girls failing to stay still for Frith's photographer. They are outside the shop of butchers and game dealers Robert, John and William Balson. Still trading, as R J Balson and Son, they now claim to be England's oldest family butchers. Further along the south side of the street (left of centre) is the Old Inn. West Court is behind the hand-cart (right).

▼ **The Almshouses 1903** 50484

Magdalene Almshouses (left), were rebuilt in 1877 on the site of a lazar-house or leper hospital, apparently founded by a member of the de Leyes or Legh family, in the early 13th century. The dedication was to St Mary Magdalene. At the time of the photograph it was for "eight deserving women" but this was reduced to four to ease overcrowding. Modernisation took place in 1955, financed by the Colfox Trust, when the number of units was increased to six. Beyond is Magdalen House (left of centre) with Old Magdalen opposite (right of centre).

▲ **General View 1909**

61641

Cottages sit beside Skilling Hill Road in a panorama eastwards across the double vales of the River Simene and the River Brit. Bridport town and St Michael's Lane (left) were largely screened by trees. The tower of St Mary's parish church peeks above them (centre). Beyond, on the horizon, is the distant shape of Shipton Hill, resembling the hull of an upturned boat (left of centre).

West Allington 1912 65056
The south side of West Allington, looking westwards from the White Lion Hotel to the Old Inn. Both pubs had landladies. Mrs Susannah Osborne was publican at the White Lion and Mrs Frances Biles at the Old Inn. The cart is outside the shop of butchers Robert John Balson and William Balson. Opposite, on the corner with North Allington, the principal towns on the cast-iron road sign are Exeter (straight ahead) and Chard (right). West Court is behind the trees.

▼ West Allington 1913 65645

This view is looking north-westwards from the junction with North Allington, at the bottom end of South Street. Lyme Regis, Axminster and Exeter are signed to the left and Chard is straight ahead, up through West Allington.

▼ From Allington Hill c1960 B207035

A Panorama south-eastwards across Allington hamlet and West Allington street to the Rope Works, St Michael's Works and Priors Mills (middle distance, left). Beyond are the gasworks and the old brewery, with Bothenhampton and West Bay in the distance. Here there is a sliver of sea (right of centre) and the plateau of the Golf Links on East Cliff.

▲ An Old Cottage 1897
40089

John Kiely's Refreshment Rooms in South Street had a rustic look, accentuated by moss on the thatched roof and the windows open for air in a hot summer. 'Accommodation for TEA PARTIES', the sign reads. 'Ginger Beer Lemonade Sold Here.' Francis Long, in Bradpole Road, was the local soft drinks manufacturer.

Victoria Grove 1897 40076
Named for the Queen and photographed in the 60th year of what had become the longest reign on record, Victoria Grove encompassed the social and architectural extremes of the era, ranging from the exuberant St Hilda's School (left) to staid town houses of the 1860s. Looking southwards through the desirable heart of the town's northern suburb, we can see No 50 further down the street (left of centre) and Nos 53 to 59 (far right) on the other side.

The Convent 1903 50486
The Visitation Convent in Pymore Road, opposite the junction with Coneygar Road, is shown here from the potato patch behind it. The boys, both day pupils and boarders, worshipped in the Roman Catholic Church in Victoria Grove. The nuns would not allow boys to use their names and instead gave each a number. Many would remember their best friends as, say, 'Six' or 'Twenty-three' for the rest of their lives. They also recalled a harsh regime in which casual correction was six strokes of a bamboo cane across the palm of the hand from the age of five onwards. The superior was Sister Mary Elizabeth. Demolition took place in 2001.

Victoria Grove and the Roman Catholic Church 1913 65642

The Roman Catholic Church (right) was built in 1845 and dedicated to St Mary and St Catherine. The Foresters' Hall is now the British Legion Hall (centre) with No 50, the prominent house behind it. The three-storey terrace of dwellings extends from No 27 (far left) to No 35.

Happy Island 1897 40097

The most romantic spot in Bridport's immediate countryside, where a public path crossed the River Asker by a narrow arched footbridge, is known as the Happy Island. Looking north-eastwards towards Bradpole, the spire of Holy Trinity can be seen on the skyline (centre). The track on the right descends from the Dorchester Road, near the junction with Lee Lane, and that to the left heads for St Andrew's Well. The delightful spot, with stream-side Spray Coppice as the backdrop (right), is in the parish of Bradpole.

Happy Island 1918 68104

Overlooking the River Asker and Happy Island, north-westwards to Watton Hill (centre) as a Great Western Railway pannier tank engine (right) steams out of Bridport Station (far left) with a goods train in the last summer of the Great War. The mixture of empty coal wagons includes (from the locomotive) 'S.M.J.' (Stratford-on-Avon and Midland Junction), 'L.Y.' (Lancashire and Yorkshire), 'M.R.' (Midland Railway), and 'G.W.' (Great Western).

Bradpole Road 1903 50482

A horseman rides north-eastwards, along what is now St Andrew's Road towards Bradpole, when this was part of that parish before boundary changes brought the northern suburbs into Bridport borough. It was provided with its own Anglican chapel of ease (right) in 1860. The dedication, to St Andrew, preserved the memory of a medieval predecessor, which gave its name to St Andrew's Well. The architect was Talbot Bury, from London, and the builders Chick and Son of Beaminster. The mason, from Bradpole, was Joseph Gibbs. The access road to the Delapre estate can be seen (left) and Rogers Cottage, beside Long's Lane, is in the distance (left of centre), with houses Nos 76 to 68 being in the near distance (right of centre).

Bradpole Road 1903 50483

Since renamed St Andrew's Road, here we are looking south-westwards towards Bridport. The nationally-known 20th-century playright Thomas Ridley Sharpe moved here from Cambridge in 1978. He resided in No 170. His farce 'Blott on the Landscape' had its television debut in 1985, with ironical timing, as the northern arm of Bridport bypass was cutting its way across meadows to the east. Here the visible semi-detached houses are No 39 (right of centre) to No 45 (far right).

Foundry Cottages 1909 61648

Foundry Cottages (left) and three-storey Foundry House (far right), in West Allington, were the hub of Richard Robert Samson's Grove Iron Works. These were the last buildings on the western edge of the town, on the Exeter road, where Foundry House is now flats and the metal-working premises of J I Blackburn Limited and an entire new housing estate has replaced the cottages. Looking eastwards towards Allington Hill (left) this view has changed almost out of all recognition.

Wykes Court 1909 61649
This is the frontage of Wykes Court when it was the home of
Major George Murray Dammer. Born in Symondsbury in 1879,
he would become one of the town's heroes of the Great War,
being part of the Yeomanry change at Agagia against the rebellious
Senussi peoples in Egypt. It won him the Military Cross and he
was painted in Lady Butler's famous picture. He went on to collect
the Distinguished Service Order for more dashing conduct on the
Mughar Ridge. Post-war he was a county councillor and a member
of the Board of Finance for the Salisbury diocese.

The Secondary School 1909 61654
Brand new, still with scaffold planks stacked behind the gate, the Secondary School in St Andrew's Road was built on land given by Lieutenant-Colonel and Mrs Thomas Alfred Colfox. It cost £5,000 and would win recognition from the Board of Education. Colonel Colfox gave more land for playing fields, in 1918, and it would then be re-designated as a Grammar School.

The Meadows c1955 B207001
Bridport's eastern suburb of Hyde, beside East Road, here looking south-eastwards from the River Asker to the pines above Walditch. Hyde Hill rises southwards (right).

West Bay

West Bay
The Quay 1897 40081
Low tide in the Basin of what was still generally known as
Bridport Harbour. Sailing vessels are grounded on their keels.
The prominent building is the George Hotel (left). This side of the
harbour had been the shipbuilding yard in Bridport creek. Elias Cox
was the last major boat-builder. Chalets would be built across the
site. The Esplanade, also behind the photographer, was paid for by
Thomas Colfox and opened in 1897 as part of the celebrations of
Queen Victoria's diamond jubilee.

West Bay, Coastguard Station 1907 58153
These are the gaunt Victorian lines of the Coastguard Station at West Bay, looking eastwards towards East Cliff, with Rocket Houses seaward from it (right). Cottages were to the left and the operational part of the building was at the seaward end. Further south, on the beach, there was an older thatched Watch House which became Old Watchouse Café.

West Bay, the Village and Beach 1922 72793
This is a detail of the chalet zone which sprang up behind the 1897-built Esplanade (right), between the waterworks and the Salt House on Pitfield Marsh (left). This was the site of medieval shipyards which were still in production into late Victorian times and launched their largest vessel, the 1,002-ton 'Speedy' for the Australia run, in 1853. Beyond, beside the George Hotel, the River Brit flows into the Basin and through the narrow Channel created between the West Pier and East Pier which project together into Lyme Bay (right). Beyond are vertical sandy strata, forming East Cliff and Burton Cliff.

West Bay, the Village and Beach 1930 83349
This view shows the esplanade (left of centre) and the twin piers protecting the channel into Bridport Harbour (right). Looking eastwards from the cliffs above Black Rock. The largest building, hip-roofed and dating from the late 19th century, is Pier Terrace (left of centre). Built as apartments it is alternatively known as Noah's Ark. Note the derrick and crane on the piers.

West Bay, the Harbourside c1955 W56052
High tide in the Basin, looking eastwards to St Andrews's Mission Church (left of centre), West Bay Hotel (centre), the Custom House (right of centre) and Old Storehouse (further right).

The Village Hinterland

Bradpole
The Village 1897 40093
Bradpole is Bridport's northern parish and suburb, and here we
are looking along Middle Street towards the 1863-built spire
of Holy Trinity church (skyline, left of centre). The village store,
which is the present Post Office (right) was advertising Venus
Soap (enamel sign on fence), Fry's Chocolate and Fry's Pure
Cocoa (windows), and Dr Sutherland's report on patent Ruta Tea
(poster in centre window). The other buildings (left to right) are
Koala Cottage, Lynn Cottage, Primrose Cottage and St George's.

Bradpole, the Village 1907 58155

The village of Bradpole is shown here from the north-east, looking south-west from above Hole House Farm and the valley of the Mangerton River across to Holy Trinity parish church (right), and the fields of St Andrew's Well (centre), to Watton Hill (middle distance, left). Beyond is the silhouette of Colmer's Hill, above Symondsbury, merging with the skyline of Quarry Hill. The churchyard (right of centre) was extended in 1817 and had filled with Victorian graves, towards the monkey puzzle tree. By mid-Edwardian times, the village was expanding into the middle distance (left).

King Charles II Stone 1912 65062

Lee Lane (left) at its junction with Dorchester Road, has a stone commemorating the escape of King Charles II after being defeated at the Battle of Worcester. He had a close call in Bridport on 23 September 1651. Erected in 1901, it quotes Thomas Fuller of Broadwindsor: "When midst your fiercest foes on every side, for your escape God did a lane provide." Twenty-one days later, Charles would reach Shoreham, Sussex, and sail to safety in France. The bulge on the horizon (right) is a hayrick.

Hyde Road 1904 52759
Leafy Hyde Road, otherwise known as Walditch Road, cuts south-eastwards through the parkland of The Hyde. This sylvan setting is only half a mile from the bustle of East Street.

▼ Walditch, the Village 1899 43879

This is a fine example of Bridport's eastern countryside, with the Dorset Downs falling away into the Marshwood Vale (far left) from the heights of Eggardon Hill and woods of Knowle Hill (left), in a panorama extending to the foothills of Shipton Hill (left). Looking north-east, from Hyde Hill, we can see Hyde in the foreground (left) and Berry Farm and Walditch hamlet in the middle distance (centre). The church of St Mary (right) was re-built in the Early English style in about 1863. It retains its original Norman font.

▼ Bothenhampton, Main Street 1904 52767

Another of the surrounding parishes into which Bridport borough expanded, Bothenhampton lies to the south-east, with a deep-cut village street which has left a dense cluster of terraces standing on distinctive raised pavements. Eastwards, it becomes Long Lane and climbs into open countryside. Looking westwards along Main Street we can see the lych-gate (at the junction) of the 1889-built Holy Trinity church, replacing a medieval building at the other end of the village. Clematis Cottage (left) faces a long line of dwellings, all of which survive, from No 5 (left end) to No 39 (far right).

▲ Bothenhampton From the South c1955
B157010

The village street at Bothenhampton (middle distance, left to right), with suburbia beyond, seen from the vicinity of Quarry Farm with an apple orchard and thatched cottages above the stream. This view is north-eastwards, towards Bridport, with Hyde Plantation glimpsed on the distant rural skyline (far right). The red-brick of Montrose, at the top of Crock Lane, is the prominent building on the skyline (left).

**Bothenhampton
The Village c1960** B157033
This is the landscape northwards from the limekilns and quarries north of Wych to the Main Street at Bothenhampton (left to right). Montrose is the distinctive red-brick house with dormer windows at the top end of Crock Lane (centre). Holy Trinity parish church is visible below it (left of centre). The pines of Hyde Plantation are on the hill behind and Hyde Hill rises eastwards (right).

▼ **Loders, General View 1903** 50495
From Boarsbarrow Hill, this view looks to St Mary's parish church and Georgian Loders Court which is the home of Viscount and Viscountess Hood (centre). The woods of Waddon rise behind. Tucked into the foreground, behind the hedge, ran the Bridport branch railway.

▼ **Loders, the Village 1903** 50496
Looking westwards along the village street from the Loders Arms (far left) we can see the Farmers' Arms Inn (centre) and trees at Loders Court, behind Church Farm House (centre). Opposite are Pound Cottage, Waynflete, Libra and Lothers (right).

▲ **Loders
The Post Office and
Village c1955** L292005
Loders Post Office, run by J A Wells, can be seen in a view eastwards from the middle of the village. Waynflete and Lothers (left) face No 41 and the Loders Arms (right of centre). The historic hexagonal post-box and the stores have since been cleared for the public house car-park.

Burton Bradstock
High Street c1955

B255099

Donkey Lane and Dormouse Cottage (right) can be seen here in the northern end of the High Street (centre) which bends to the west beside Pound House (centre) to become Barr Lane as it carries the main road towards Bridport. The Anchor Inn is around the corner and a range of 17th-century cottages are opposite. Bramble Cottage, below the telegraph pole (left), has a 'For Sale' sign in the window. Next-door is Lilac Cottage.

Burton Bradstock
The Village 1902 48412
This photograph looks northwards up the High Street to Donkey
Lane and the 17th-century thatched Dormouse Cottage on the
corner (centre). Other old cottages are opposite, from the Old
Apple Barn (far left) and Little Thatches to Bramble Cottage. Pound
House is behind the telegraph pole. The 1879-dated Reading Room
is down the street from Rock House (right of centre), with the
gable-end of the Three Horseshoes in the foreground (far right).
Its enamelled sign is for Colman's Mustard. A poster beside the
door carries the crown and 'E R' initials for the new King, Edward
Rex, proclaiming 'Recruits Wanted' for the armed forces. Retired
fishermen stand in the road.

Burton Bradstock, the Village 1922 72819
Northwards along Middle Street, a 17th-century thatched cottage stands on the corner with Grove Road (centre). Ingram House (left) is of a similar date but has been much altered. The Red House stands opposite, in ivy-clad brick (right). A stone wall (far right) is the gable-end of the 1635-dated White House.

Burton Bradstock, the Village c1955 B255047
Taken from the bridge over the River Bride, this view looks northwards into the southern section of the High Street. Bridge Stores (right of centre) advertises Colman's Mustard in much more basic style than the Victorian sign that used to look down on the central part of the street. A figure (disappearing right) is entering the Recreation Ground. The Three Horseshoes public house is behind the parked cars (centre).

Swyre, The Bull Inn c1965 S813051

Marking the end of an era, the Bull Inn at Swyre was one of the last roadhouses to be built in England in the 1930s, enabling Mrs Bessie Case to offer 'hotel accommodation' in time for Defence Area status and use by the 1st Infantry Division of the United States Army later in the Second World War. Her telephone number was Burton Bradstock 50. Architecturally, the building is more typical of arterial roads, rather than that expected beside the B3157 coast road (bottom right), a mile inland from the western end of the Chesil Beach.

Puncknowle, the Village 1906 54548

This is a low-angle shot up Church Street from beneath the horse chestnut trees in the churchyard (right) to the thatched Crown Inn (centre). The bay windows with decorative tiles are on Durban Cottage and Thornleigh Cottage. The girls are on the steps of No 1 of the three Burwell Cottages. The village name, incidentally, is pronounced as "Punnel".

▲ Puncknowle The Water-cart c1955

P120001

Remote parts of Dorset were not connected to mains water until the 1960s. Looking east from the western end of the village, we can see the road junction beside what has become a single Burwell Cottage (centre). Rectory Lane used to be called Duck Street. The water-carter (right) has just drawn water from the spout and trough recessed in the wall (far right). Unpasteurised milk was also delivered around the village in the same way until 1962. Manor Cottage is opposite (left).

**Shipton Gorge
The Village 1899**
43880
Taken from the
eastern end of
the village, above
Burbitt Lane. This
view looks north-
eastwards to
St Martin's parish
church (right), and
the distinctive
599-feet profile of
Shipton Hill (centre).
There are several
privies half-way up
the back gardens
(left).

Powerstock, the Village 1902 48417
This view was taken from Nettlecombe looking towards the thatched Knapp House and St Mary's parish church (centre). Beside it, dwarfed by a huge sycamore tree, are the thatched Three Horseshoes Inn and tiled Way Cottage (left of centre). The modern houses (left) are down towards Merriott Bridge. Dugberry Hill is on the skyline (right of church tower).

Powerstock, the Village c1960 P233007
Up School Hill, northwards from Merriott, the sign of the Three Horseshoes can be seen in the distance. Brookview is the house with Powerstock Primary School behind it (left of centre) and Sunnyside is further up the hill.

Melplash
The Village 1912 65063
South Warren Hill rises to form the skyline in this picture, taken from the highway between Rose Cottage (left) and Rock Cottage (right). Lilac Cottage and what is now Coryates are hidden in the trees behind them. Spring Cottage (centre) subsequently became a garage.

**Netherbury
The Village 1902** 48440
North-eastwards from
Japonica Cottage,
housing the Post Office
(left), the photographer
centres on the 1839-built
Congregational Chapel.
Opposite is Worcester
Cottage and Chantry Walk
(right). The railings of
The Redes form the other
corner (near right) of the
village crossroads.

Melplash, the Village 1907 58146
A delivery cart from Hine Brothers, butchers in Beaminster, is seen here in the main street at Melplash. Looking southwards along the main road towards Bridport, Rock Cottage and Groom's Cottage face the thatched Rose Cottage on the right.

Netherbury the Village 1912 65066
From this view of the crossroads, one can see The Redes on the left, and on the right, Japonica Cottage, which housed Netherbury Post Office.

Netherbury The Village c1955
N9024
Looking north-westwards from Lower Yonderover Farm, with hay-bales in Mill House paddock (foreground) and the sign for the Star Inn (centre), the River Brit skirts the edge of the meadow (left to right). Star Cottages (right of centre) are now Gemini Cottages.

◄ **Symondsbury, the Village c1955** S246002

Mark Twain expected his perfect piece of England to have a castle and the odd ruin. Here Symondsbury may be deficient but it can boast the thatched Ilchester Arms Inn (right), which is named for the Strangways family, owning lands from Abbotsbury Swannery to Melbury House. Looking north, from the lane into the village from Miles Cross, 1868-dated Symondsbury School and tower of St John's Church in the background can be seen.

Symondsbury
The Village and Church 1899
43871

"This England", as Mark Twain described "that beauty which is England alone – it has no duplicate". This beautiful view, seen from the path up the hill towards Miles Cross, looks north to the Manor House (top left) and its thatched 17th-century barn (right of centre). The closer buildings are the Rectory (left), parish church of St John the Baptist (centre), and the school (middle right). Trees of The Grove extend south-westwards (left) and Old Warren Hill forms the horizon.

Symondsbury
The Ilchester Arms and
Church c1955 S246007

A closer view of the Ilchester Arms Inn. It is one of the oldest buildings in the area, dating from the 16th century, with five bays of original timbering including curved trusses and wind-braces as well as inglenook fireplaces and exposed beams. The notice above the side door (right) tells us that the publican was Ernest Norris, licensed to sell beer and cider, with the latter still being produced locally into the new millennium.

Morecombelake
Old Cottages 1904
52773

A rustic corner, with mossy thatch and a corrugated-iron porch lid, lies beside Loves Lane on the western slope of Hardown Hill. Looking south-westwards towards Stonebarrow Hill, the Forge and Blacksmith's Cottage can be seen on the left and a range of old thatched cottages rise from the Old Post Office (centre).

▼ **Chideock, the Village 1897** 40091
The houses in this view are (starting with the closest):
Gate Cottage, Fernley, Hill View and the thatched Park
Farmhouse. The George Inn is further along on the left.

▼ **Chideock, the Village 1903** 50488
Further west along Main Street, looking towards Lyme Regis, the plateau of
Langdon Hill forms the skyline (centre). The cart is beside Rose Cottage and Foss
Cottage (left). James Foss, who died in 1902, bequeathed £200 towards the
upkeep of the parish church. Opposite are The Farmery (centre), Japonica Cottage,
and Lilac Cottage (right).

▲ **Chideock
The Village 1922** 65078
Carter and cart-horse are
climbing Main Street in a
view looking westwards
towards Langdon Hill
(centre). Behind them
is the gable-end of
the Farmery and Hope
Cottage (right of centre).
Japonica Cottage (right of
telegraph pole) has 16th-
century stone mullioned
windows. Lilac Cottage
is next (right). Ashford
Cottage is opposite (left)
and Rose Cottage is
below it (left of centre).

Chideock, the Village 1903 50489
Battlemented parapets of the 15th-century nave and porch of St Giles parish church are seen here on the corner with North Road (left). This picture looks eastwards down Main Street to Quarry Hill (left) and Eype Down (right). Next down the street (left of centre) is the Castle Inn which was rebuilt by Sir Frederick Weld after a fire in 1887, with Chideock House below it. Opposite, the stone and slate cottages are Trefoil and Corner Cottage, on Stocks Corner, where Duck Street turns towards Seatown hamlet, beside Lyme Bay. The Clock House completes the scene (far right).

Chideock
Main Street 1912 65079
Chideok House on the left, was, at this time, known as Myrtle Cottage,
with a Mrs Bindloss as its inhabitant. Beyond are an obscured Bridge
Cottage, By the Stream, and Apple Tree Thatch (centre). Opposite
are Chapel Cottage, Chideock Court, Alice Cottage, and Chideock
Post Office (far right). The enamelled sign over the door offers the
services of the day: 'Post Office for Money Order, Savings Bank, Parcel
Post, Telegraph, Insurance and Annuity Business'. Mrs Gibbs, the
postmistress, stands in the doorway with daughter Hilda. In the street
is Mrs Kate Foss with Kathleen Mary Foss, holding everyone's attention,
in the pram. The latter would marry Wilf Symes and become the village
postmistress. The Symes family still run Chideock Post Office Stores
further down the street.

Chideock, the Village 1922 72804
Another view of Chideock Post Office (right), looking eastwards to Mervyn House, Staddlestones, and Rose Cottage (centre). The shadowy side of the street rises from Chapel Cottage and Chideock Court (with the vintage car parked beside its railings) to Alice Cottage and what is now the Old Post Office.

Chideock, Horse and Cart 1922 65080X
A rustic scene in the centre of the village, southwards along Duck Street, with the Swiss Cottage contributing its flamboyantly flowing thatch (left). This is the junction with Mill Lane (left of centre) beside Roadstead House (right). Seahill Lane bends to the right, towards Seatown.

Western Coast

Seatown
the Hamlet and Beach 1922 72810
A classic west Dorset view, showing Seatown and Golden Cap which, at
618 feet above sea level, is the highest cliff on the South Coast of England. Langdon Hill can
be seen on the skyline (right of centre) at the heart of what is now the Golden Cap Estate of
the National Trust. Here the River Winniford trickles through the shingle into the sea. Note
the beach-huts on the landslipped cliff. The closest building to the water was the thatched
Fishermen's Hut (left of centre) with the tiled Anchor Inn and thatched Anchor Cottages
next (centre) and the Coastguard Station behind. The flagpole, with a yard-arm, was used to
send signals. Staff lived in the four Guard House Cottages (right of centre). The veranda is
on Seatown Villa (right).

Seatown, The Anchor Inn 1930 83364
This view was taken looking westwards from a packhorse bridge over the River Winniford. By now the Fishermen's Hut has gone, but the other buildings look much the same, from the Anchor Inn (left) and Anchor Cottages to the Coastguard Station, Guard House Cottages, and Seatown Villa. Golden Cap, looming above, is a mile away.

Eype, the Village 1899 43872
A tiny coastal hamlet in the parish of Symondsbury, Eype was provided with its own 350-seat chapel of ease, dedicated to St Peter, in 1865 (right-hand skyline). This view is from the lower slopes of Thorncombe Beacon, looking north-east, to Lower Eype Farm (left) and Lower Eype hamlet (centre), with the adjacent farmstead of Bonville (right). Mount Lane climbs the hill towards St Peter's Church on The Mount (right of centre).

▼ **Eype, the Village 1930** 83370
This is another view of Lower Eype from further to the south-west, closer to the
cliff above Lyme Bay, looking inland to Mount Lane and St Peter's Church (centre).
The top of the same iron-railed gate as in the 1899 photograph (43872) can be
seen in the hedge in the foreground. In the 1930s, Albert Lee was running the
Post Office in Lower Eype and Thomas Lee was the farmer. Charles and
William Warren were boatmen and Robert Warren quarried sand and sold
shingle from the beach to the south.

▼ **Eype, Edgecliff Camp c1955** E54002
A small-scale start for what is now Highlands End Caravan Park. here we are
Looking north towards St Peter's Church, on The Mount. The original Edgecliff
name was dropped because it sounded dangerous. Actually, the site lies 500 yards
inland and is a field away from the coastal path.

▲ **Eype, the Village c1955**
E54053
This view was taken
from below the New Inn,
looking down into lower
Eype from Mount Lane.
The 1860-dated plaque
is on Eype School (far
left). Cottages on the
other side rise from Lea
Cottage (left of centre),
to the terrace comprising
Hydrangea Cottage,
Clematis Cottage,
Rosemary Cottage and
Sunset Cottage (beside
the telephone kiosk).

Eype
The Post Office c1955
E54028
Looking westwards into
the idyllic cul-de-sac,
hydrangeas are in bloom
beside Vine Cottage (right).
Beyond, then housing the
Post Office, is Journey's
End, which takes its name
from local landowner
R C Sherriff's best-known
play. Duck's Bottom is
behind The Chalet (top left).

Eype, the Beach 1930 83371

This view shows Eype Mouth, looking westwards to what is now a National Trust skyline, with Ridge Cliff and Doghouse Hill rising into the 508-feet summit of Thorncombe Beacon (centre). Below, from Hope Corner to the stream that trickles beside the rowing boat, the beach was also donated to the Trust by playwright Robert Cedric Sherriff in 1966. The lands of Downhouse Farm ended beside the chalet and the boathouse, which was used by the Warren family in the 1930s. Its place in history was the disappearance out to sea of William Powell MP, the member for Malmesbury, in a run-away balloon after an aborted clifftop landing on 10 December 1881.

Eype, Eype Mouth 1930 83372

A moody shot of Charles and William Warren's boathouse at Eype Mouth, southwards across Lyme Bay. Crab, lobster and crayfish pots are stacked by the door. The stream disappears into the pebbles (left) and a moderate sea is running in what is visibly unsettled weather.

Index

FRITH PRODUCTS & SERVICES

Francis Frith would doubtless be pleased to know that the pioneering publishing venture he started in 1860 still continues today. Over a hundred and forty years later, The Francis Frith Collection continues in the same innovative tradition and is now one of the foremost publishers of vintage photographs in the world. Some of the current activities include:

INTERIOR DECORATION

Today Frith's photographs can be seen framed and as giant wall murals in thousands of pubs, restaurants, hotels, banks, retail stores and other public buildings throughout the country. In every case they enhance the unique local atmosphere of the places they depict and provide reminders of gentler days in an increasingly busy and frenetic world.

PRODUCT PROMOTIONS

Frith products are used by many major companies to promote the sales of their own products or to reinforce their own history and heritage. Frith promotions have been used by Hovis bread, Courage beers, Scots Porage Oats, Colman's mustard, Cadbury's foods, Mellow Birds coffee, Dunhill pipe tobacco, Guinness, and Bulmer's Cider.

GENEALOGY AND FAMILY HISTORY

As the interest in family history and roots grows world-wide, more and more people are turning to Frith's photographs of Great Britain for images of the towns, villages and streets where their ancestors lived; and, of course, photographs of the churches and chapels where their ancestors were christened, married and buried are an essential part of every genealogy tree and family album.

FRITH PRODUCTS

All Frith photographs are available Framed or just as Mounted Prints and unmounted versions. These may be ordered from the address below. Other products available are - Calendars, Jigsaws, Canvas Prints, Mugs, Tea Towels, Tableware and local and prestige books.

THE INTERNET

Over several hundred thousand Frith photographs can be viewed and purchased on the internet through the Frith websites!

For more detailed information on Frith products, look at
www.francisfrith.com

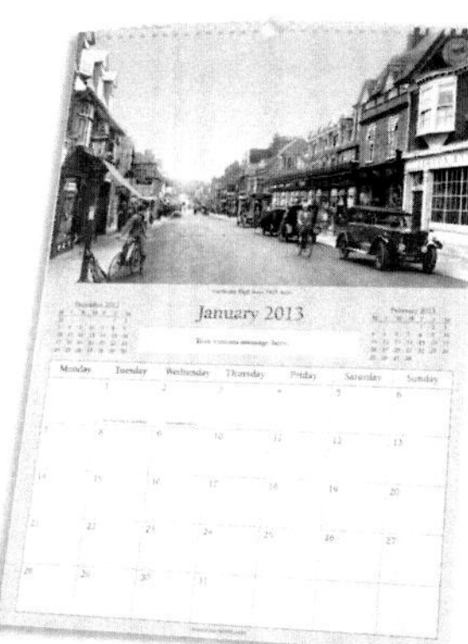

See the complete list of Frith Books at: www.francisfrith.com

This web site is regularly updated with the latest list of publications from The Francis Frith Collection. If you wish to buy books relating to another part of the country that your local bookshop does not stock, you may purchase on-line.

For further information, trade, or author enquiries please contact us at the address below:

The Francis Frith Collection, Unit 19 Kingsmead Business Park, Gillingham, Dorset SP8 5FB.

Tel: +44 (0)1722 716 376   Email: sales@francisfrith.co.uk

See Frith products on the internet at www.francisfrith.com

FREE PRINT OF YOUR CHOICE
CHOOSE A PHOTOGRAPH FROM THIS BOOK

+ POSTAGE

Mounted Print
Overall size 14 x 11 inches (355 x 280mm)

TO RECEIVE YOUR FREE PRINT

Choose any Frith photograph in this book

Simply complete the Voucher opposite and return it with your payment (to cover postage and handling) and we will print the photograph of your choice in SEPIA (size 11 x 8 inches) and supply it in a cream mount ready to frame (overall size 14 x 11 inches).

Order additional Mounted Prints at HALF PRICE - £19.00 each (normally £38.00)

If you would like to order more Frith prints from this book, possibly as gifts for friends and family, you can buy them at half price (with no additional postage costs).

Have your Mounted Prints framed

For an extra £20.00 per print you can have your mounted print(s) framed in an elegant polished wood and gilt moulding, overall size 16 x 13 inches (no additional postage required).

IMPORTANT!

❶ Please note: aerial photographs and photographs with a reference number starting with a "Z" are not Frith photographs and cannot be supplied under this offer.

❷ Offer valid for delivery to one UK address only.

❸ These special prices are only available if you use this form to order. You must use the ORIGINAL VOUCHER on this page (no copies permitted). We can only despatch to one UK address.

❹ This offer cannot be combined with any other offer.

As a customer your name & address will be stored by Frith but not sold or rented to third parties. Your data will be used for the purpose of this promotion only.

Send completed Voucher form to:

**The Francis Frith Collection,
1 Chilmark Estate House, Chilmark,
Salisbury, Wiltshire SP3 5DU**

Voucher for **FREE** and Reduced Price Frith Prints

Please do not photocopy this voucher. Only the original is valid, so please fill it in, cut it out and return it to us with your order.

Picture ref no	Page no	Qty	Mounted @ £19.00	Framed + £20.00	Total Cost £
		1	Free of charge*	£	£
			£19.00	£	£
			£19.00	£	£
			£19.00	£	£
			£19.00	£	£
			£19.00	£	£

Please allow 28 days for delivery. Offer available to one UK address only

* Post & handling		£3.80
Total Order Cost		£

Title of this book . . . .

I enclose a cheque/postal order for £ . . . .
made payable to 'Heritage Resource Management Ltd'

OR please debit my Mastercard / Visa / Maestro card, details below

Card Number:

Issue No (Maestro only):   Valid from (Maestro):

Card Security Number: Expires:

Signature:

Name Mr/Mrs/Ms ....

Address ....

....

....

.... Postcode ....

Daytime Tel No ....

Email ....

Valid to 31/12/26

Free Print – see overleaf